STAKE SCIENCE
PLEASURE'S

Dr. Henrietta Abbey

Stake Science Pleasure's
Copyright © 2026 by Dr. Henrietta Abbey

ISBN: 979-8-9999034-3-3 (Paperback)
       979-8-9999034-4-0 (Hardback)
       979-8-9999034-5-7 (E-book)

Library of Congress Control Number:
Published By:

MISSION MASS MIMEO

Publisher Provider:

BOOKMARC
ALLIANCE

BookmarcAlliance
California, USA

www.bookmarcalliance.com

CONTENTS

CHAPTER ONE

There are 383 different Wall Streets known in modern world, but the historical one in Manhattan, New York City is the famous of them all. It is surrounded by past myths dated back to the 17th century. From time, it has fully developed to become a financial settlement recognized in New York and in the world. As money is very essential to the human needs so is Wall Street important to New Yorkers and investors. It is also called the Financial District. Although very popular, it is hidden to deter fraud activities and terrorists; in that only New Yorkers, investor, the rich and the affluent are familiar with its massive development and money investments. To invest in Wall Street, you need not stay or work in that area. However, people who live or work in the area have become infested with the area and in investing thereby acquiring wealth in one way or the other.

Wall Street area also has harbor labor movements such as the Tea Party Movement and Occupy Wall Street. From authors such as Steve Fraser in his book 'Wall Street' he says the nation has wrestled, and still wrestles with fundamental questions of wealth and work, democracy and elitism, greed and salvation all from this famous district Wall Street. Most of Wall Street workers in the stock market work on contracts. However, some of the clerks, cleaners and security workers belong to unions. They have what we call clerical workers union. Just as 32BJ represents doormen, cleaners and other fields of workers, people are working in Wall Street who belongs to unions. Also, some companies in the area belong to unions. Some hotels in the area have workers belonging to a union. Mostly the lowest paid workers do belong to a union or temp agencies where they are dispersed to the Wall Street offices to work.

Today all you need is to get on the computer and the internet to make transactions. Previously, transacts were done by hand and in person. People born in New York City who wants to make it big in the future automatically learn of the place one way or the other, and tap into wealth in the area as they grow with the knowledge of Wall Street. Many interviews show that the working class and the rich people living and working in the area are well to do. They happen to manage their finances better and know more about cash compare to folks who do not socialize with the place nor become familiar with the area. It is an expensive place to live and to work. Wall Street runs from East of Broadway to the South Street on the East River, through the historical center of the Financial District, and its surroundings. It is the first home of the New York Stock Exchange and the headquarters of most financial institutions and financial industry. Some of the U.S. stock exchanges in Wall Street are NYSE, NASDAQ, AMEX, NYMEX, and NYBOT. Also, Wall Street was known as the "House of Morgan," and its bank headquarters in the area were known to address American finance as a whole.

CHAPTER TWO

Even though, wealth associated with the area, there has been ups and down in the area. There have been times when the market became so low that people withdrew from investing. In the 21st century, the economy grew so bad in the USA that investors felt inclined to take their money from the market. For instance, there was a case of Ponce Scheme where the investor used other investors' money for his gain, and people lost a great deal of money. This scheme led to subsequent suicide and death of individuals who were prey to these circumstances. On September 16, 1920, a bomb exploded in front of the headquarters of J.P. Morgan Inc. at 23 Wall Street, killing 38 people and injuring 300 people. Folks crowded on Wall Street and Broad Street where the crash occurred. After twenty years of investigation, it is still a mystery as to who was behind the bombing of September 1920. The FBI rendered the case inactive in 1940.

On September 11, terrorist also bombed the financial district killing many people in the area and causing New York finances to dwindle. The attack left somewhat of an architectural void as new developments since the 1970's have played off the complex aesthetically. It contributed to the loss of business on Wall Street, due to temporary to permanent relocation to New Jersey and further decentralization with establishments transferred to cities like Chicago, Denver, and Boston. In effect, the economy has been severely affected, and prices have gone high. Thanks to the President for creating an anti-terrorist team to fight off future attacks. Hence there is always a bomb search in areas of high crime activities. It so happened that these bombs occurred in the month of September but different years. In 1929 the stock market crashed which was termed the "Great Crash." The economy plunged into great depression. New development of the Financial District stagnated.

CHAPTER THREE

There are lots of historical myths surrounding the place. According to history, in the 17th century, Wall Street used to be a northern boundary of the New Amsterdam settlement. In 1640 the Dutch built a fence around the plot and residence of the colony. Later on, Peter Stuyvesant thought it great to construct a stronger stockade to help trade is slaves. The wall built was 12 foot of timber and earth created in 1653 with strong palisades. The barrier created and strengthened over time. It also served as a defense against attack from various Native American tribes. In 1685 surveyors built Wall Street alongside the stockade. The wall was broken down by the Government in 1699. The word "wall" adopted from the original Dutch as the name for the area and a street was name after the wall. The word "wal" in Dutch means fortification. As time went on the area became noted for the financial settlement. The name wall became suitability to fortify New York wealth and its finances. During the 18th century, there used to be a buttonwood tree at the foot of Wall Street under which traders and speculators would gather to trade informally. In 1792, the traders formed the association called Buttonwood Agreement which used to be the original New York Stock Exchange. In 1789, the first presidential inauguration of George Washington taking the oath of office on the balcony of Federal Hall which overlooked the Wall Street on April 30, 1789; the location known as the passing of the Bill of Rights. In 1889, the Wall Street Journal became official. It was named after the actual street. Currently, the journal has become an international influence in daily business newspapers published in New York City. It is second in circulation in the United States today. Rupert Murdoch's News Corp owns it since 2007.

CHAPTER FOUR

It is said that Wall Street's Culture is rigid and many people criticized it. It old stereotype stemming from the fact that people associated with Wall Street want to protect their interest. It is also linked to the WASP establishment. Some habits include drinking of coffee, walking most of the time briskly, and dressing in suits mostly of dark colors whether rain or shine; Wall Street establishments resist government oversights and rules. Although New York City has a reputation of being bureaucratic, people in Wall Street are so stiff that it is difficult for middle-class entrepreneurs to live and work in that area and to do business over there. In most cases, people associated with Wall Street have become famous with their reputations limited to members of the stock brokerage and banking communities. Most people gained national and international fame through stocks. Others earned their fame through investment strategies, financing, reporting, legal or regulatory sills. Some also are remembered for their greed. The Charging Bull Sculpture by Arturo Di Modica is one of the most iconic representations of the market prosperity in the area. It represents boom and bull market economy. Initially, the bull was placed in front of the New York Stock Exchange but moved to its current location on Bowling Green. Wall Street also represents financial and economic power. It also represents elitism and political power because money can buy lots of things. Wall Street has become a symbol of a country with economic system developing not through colonialism and plunder. It strife's on trade, capitalism, and innovation

The architectural building in the area is of the gilded age with art deco in the neighborhood. Landmark buildings on Wall Street are the Federal Hall, 14 Wall Street which is Bankers Trust Company building, 40 Wall Street, The Trump building and the already mentioned New York Stock Exchange at the corner of Broad Street. There is a Postal Service also in that area. The older skyscrapers built with elaborate facades. The buildings in the area are tall and dark in color. They also served as a defense and a cover-up in the area because of the waters in that area; in that visitors cannot quickly determine the beauty of the city until they enter within. When you walk through Wall Street, you seem lost among the tall gigantic buildings. Most of the buildings have modern windows. Some of the windows are small others significant. The buildings built annex each other. There are lots of companies housing these buildings. There are apartments in the area however, they are costly. Most of the workers in the area commute from different parts of the country, state and the city to the area. In the mornings the area is crowded for its small and narrow street. The people are more, and the road looks small to hold the crowd. Besides, the street sometimes blocked on Broadway, and a lot of mini pillars and stands have been constructed on Wall Street making the space available for pedestrians limited. Some people travel from far to come and live in the area to trade in stocks. Most of the buildings modified. Most of the brick buildings have been replaced by pilasters, columns, and steels. There is much demolishing going on in that area. New ones are replacing old buildings. There isn't a lot of fire outbreak so most of the buildings are secured and intact. The rain does not cause the most damage because the outer walls and environment are achieved. There are no houses in that area only offices, co-ops, condominiums and apartments.

The streets are narrow and slim. When you walk there during the day, all you hear is the air condition sound during the daytime. Sometimes you see streams of steam coming out of the drainage system. Some of the streets have been dug several times leaving an uneven mark on the tardy road. In winter, it is cold because of the water. It is normally freezing. You see lots of people with heavy coats and professional attires in the area. Most of the women wear heels, and a few wear dressing sneakers. Most of their attires are dark in color especially during the winter and the fall. During the summer, they preferred to wear light bright colors however the dress code does not change. They still maintain the professional touch. They look smart in the working gears. It's only a few that wore sports clothing as a knock about in the area. Most people are nicely and neatly dressed. Most of the people seen in the area are whites from different parts of the world. During the night, and the weekends, the place is tranquil. It is like a ghost town.

There are restaurants and shops on Wall Street. Some Indian restaurants, Pizzerias shops, Italian restaurants, few Mexican and Spanish restaurant; some fast food; I never saw a grocery shop in the area as we have in the Bronx such as Ctown, Mets supermarket and Associates supermarket. I gather that most of them buy cooked food. There was only one Gourmet restaurant on Wall Street. There are few mini-shops in the area. There are no African restaurants. From time to time, farmers gather on Bowling Green to sell inorganic and organic products. Buying food in the area is expensive. A drink alone cost a dollar seventy-five cents.

There is clothing and accessories store called Bolton's on Wall Street and Water Street. Also, there is one departmental store in the area called Century 21. It is a departmental store founded in 1961. The retail store sells clothing, footwear, beddings, furniture, jewelry, beauty products, electronics, and house wares. During the holidays their products are cheaper. There are other stores in the immediate area. Some of these individual stores sell expensive items. Only a few of these stores sell moderately because of the area, items are expensive. During the summer products such as clothing and footwear are less expensive. Some of the retail stores do not last long. They relocate now and then. Also, new stores are opened in the area now and then. The postal service in the area is always crowded. There is a long line because most of the people worked during business hours and the postal service opened during business hours, many people cramp into the post office to buy stamps, money orders, process business mails and to do what they got to do at the postal service like changing of address, forwarding mails and so forth.

CHAPTER FIVE

The means of transportation to Wall Street are diverse. There is the Staten Island Ferry to the East South of Wall Street commuting people to and from Staten Island. Initially, the fare was one dollar. As time went on the place was re-developed, and the fare dropped. Now it is free to board the Staten Island Ferry. There is a Waterway on South Street. The Waterways commute people from Long Island, New Jersey, Staten Island, and Upstate. Also, Grey Hound buses are located on South Street very close to the waterway, which carries people to other states. The number four and five train stops on Broadway and Wall Street. The number two and three train stops on Wall Street and Pearl Street. The number J, M, and Z trains stop on Wall Street and Broad Street. The number one train stops a little far from Wall Street on Rector Street. The bus M15 runs from Water Street area to the Staten Island Terminal. These descriptions show how vital the street is and the number of people that use the road and inhabit the area. For a small street starting on East Broadway to South

Street, a maximum of ten blocks, it is impressive. The South Seaport is also two blocks away from Wall Street. There are ships from different parts of the world that stay and dock in the area, bring visitors and travelers who come flooding to the city. On the South Seaport, they have an area designated for entertainment. There, the community holds meetings, have fun activities and fun-fares. The seaport area is picturesque scenery where lovers walk, meet and take pictures, and for romantic get-away. Also, there are lots of film shootings on Wall Street and the surrounding areas.

CHAPTER SIX

On September 17 2011, protesters calling themselves Occupy Wall Street did occupy Zuccotti Parks which is in the confines of the Financial District and disrupting business and the Wall Street Market. From the financial districts, the movement grew to cover other parts of America and Europe with currently 95 cities participating in the move across the United States and 82 Countries also involved. Over 600 communities in America included. The movement is in place to fight for social and economic inequality in the system and to protest for the creation of jobs for students and graduates. Among other things that the movement would want the president to solve is student loans with the increasingly high percentage rate. The reason, I am talking about the move is because it started in Wall Street area, just as Stock and Bonds from Wall Street has gained world attention, so as Occupy Wall Street Movement gained global recognition. Unions like the SEIU, DC 37 and PSC support Occupy Wall Street and give funds and donations in favor of the movement.

The movement faced much opposition from the police. Some jailed while the beat others. It even came on news that one captain was videotaped striking a protestor. That captain was not able to defend his actions and issued disciplinary actions. This issue reminds me of the Haymarket killing in our textbooks. From the textbook, 'From the folks who brought you the weekend" it tells of the story of picketing in Haymarket Square that the police beat the protesters and some killed. After that, they built a statue twice to remember the occasion but were destroyed twice because the statue was that of a policeman. In Occupy Wall Street, some of the protestors even married at the place to seal the bond of the movement, and it was in the newspaper. Zuccotti Park remains an iconic place just as Haymarket Square remain an historical area (page 126).

CHAPTER SEVEN

Wall Street controls the economy. Even though Wall Street per say do not participate in Unions, there are businesses in the area that join unions and some of their workers who are paid less wages belong to unions. "For over a decade Wall Street has enjoyed an incestuous and exploitative relationship with the public sector Unions because employee pension funds have poured more new money into their equities markets than any other single source" (Internet, 2012). Also there are union workers such as city workers who invest through 401k, 457 and pension. If Wall Street booms our investments will increases, if not then investors lose and it affects the economy. Therefore, union workers are currently keen on what goes on in Wall Street. Also there are individual workers who physically buy the stocks and bonds without using the pension system or the 401k or the 457 plan. Some of these individual workers work in Wall Street area and beyond, others are workers who are in unions, others are non-union workers. Wall Street affects labor. They hire people in the area to make business and money.

According to historian Steve Fraser, "Wall Street, after all, was the quintessential capitalist institution. Or was it? In so far as it lubricated the mechanisms of trade and investment, yes it was. But as a cultivator of the moral virtues Ford and many others prized it inspired grave doubts." (Fraser, 139). He continued to say that, "After the Civil War, however, the conundrum of wealth and poverty in the rapidly industrializing economy commanded everyone's attention. And in a debate that ranged from the pulpit to the Broadway Theater. Wall Street came to occupy a distinctive niche within the American psyche. America's Gilded Age got its name, in part, thanks to spectacularly ostentatious displays of wealth by a nouveau-riche class of financiers and industrialists. Their extravagance was especially noisome because it coincided with a time of urban and rural squalor, poverty, and desperation so immense that no one in the New World had seen anything like it before." (Fraser, 150-151). "By the 1990's many people, whose Depression-era mothers and fathers might cringe at the very thought of wagering anything on the stock market, had come to see it as an entirely reasonable place not only to make provision for their retirement but to finance college educations, a wedding, vacation homes, and ordinary big-ticket consumer items." (Fraser, 178).

Low-income workers are beginning to get interested in investing in Wall Street in various ways. Low-income workers through social networks and education are learning about investing and taking chances to invest for the future. The question is does the size of low-income workers social networks influence the chances of them investing in Wall Street? And what are factors that influence low-income workers chances of investing in Wall Street? Because low-income workers are stretched financially, they do not have enough money for extra financial activities, therefore, it is difficult for them to save. However, low-income workers are beginning to rely on some savings such as pensions, investment funds, 401k and 457 as a means of saving towards their retirement and as a source of a second income. Some ways in which they get their motivation to invest is through education, and interaction with friends, co-workers, family, and experienced investors in Wall Street. Various literature reviews show that low-income workers invest when they come into contact with a third variable. It has come to the notice of the general public that, low-income workers who have large social networks in Wall Street are more inclined to invest than low-income workers with small social networks in Wall Street. Policymakers are interested in low-income response to investment because they want to find ways of helping low income workers save towards retirement and have adequate money so that they do not fall on welfare.

Also, they want to minimize the size of low-income workers who are recipients of welfare and welfare recipients will not be a burden to the government.

CHAPTER EIGHT

According to four journal articles extracted from the internet, education, race, risk tolerance and socio-cultural rich background of an environment play roles in investing especially in Wall Street. Individuals are motivated by social network, education and continuous acquiring of information to investors. Rui, Gutter, and Hanna (2010) state that blacks and Hispanics are less likely to take risks in investment compared to whites who are more likely to take risks when it comes to investing. Blacks and Hispanics will take risks when they have full understanding of the process of investing and have reliable source of information, other source of income and support; and have the understanding of what it means to have extra income through investing. Rui, Gutter and Hanna (2010) are of the view that government agencies and financial institutions should educate more blacks and Hispanics on investing and to show them all techniques involved in investing. Currently, researchers were trying to answer risk tolerance of whites, blacks and Hispanics. The results were that 59% of whites,

43% of blacks and 36% of Hispanics were more likely to take risks when it comes to investing.

Also, to invest, the individual weighs the pros and cons involved in investment. The investor thinks of the present versus the future. Should he or she spend money on other things and forget about the future or should he or she invest now, to plan for future? These are some of the factors that investors take into consideration before investing. Blacks and Hispanics who earn less money, will find it hard to depart with the little they have unless controlled by second income or other source of income. Also, Nagy and Obenberger (1994) argue that expressed investors are "completely rational, able to deal with complex choices, risk-averse and wealth-maximizing" because of their educational background. AS researchers were studying retail investors' behavior and what motivate them to invest, they found that investors do not rely on single integrated approach to investing. They take many factors into consideration when investing plus a large social interaction among investors help in making good choices.

Thirdly an example of experience investors attitudes are shown in an Indian setting where the economy is bad because of political anarchy, bombarding and misconception and cold calculation of financial wizards in India, investors in the country have developed a high-risk tolerance which helps in fighting the ups and downs of the fluctuating market. The researcher trying to answer discrepancies in investing in India; found that, investors make ration decisions. That they are unbiased in future predictions of stock and those researchers found that investors could also be irrational and make predictable error about their returns in investment. Based on a survey by Sultana (2010), discovered that the individuals prefer to invest in financial products which give risk-free returns. Indians prefer to play safe in investing if you control for they high salaries, income and education. He also found out that there is relationship between gender, age and risk tolerance level of individual investors among Indians.

Fourthly a community such as Wall Street also have ups and downs as reported in India however because it is a money making area, people who work and live in Wall Street have also developed a high-risk tolerance behavior against bad economy. The socio-cultural system cherishes money making as a strong orientation (Sjoberg, 2004) and has helped built a lot of financial stability. Sjoberg started by answering the question, why does Wall Street have a strong financial background. Sjoberg, discovered that from generation to generation, past investors pass on their wealth and experience in investing to friends and family and they use that as a source of stronghold.

Their talk of the day and communication is all about money. The community is always conscious about money and money making, making the area the most famous financial district in the world.

CHAPTER NINE

On October 29th a tropical storm hit New York City. The storm caused floods in the streets, tunnels and subways cutting power in and around the city (Wikipedia, 2013). It was estimated that the damage alone was over 68 billion USD in June 2012 (Wikipedia, 2013). About 286 people were killed due to the storm in the 7 countries affected (Wikipedia, 2013). The unusual merger of the storm caused it to be nicknamed "Superstorm Sandy" by the media and organizations of the U.S. government. Initially, the storm started developing as a tropical wave from the Western Caribbean Sea on October 22 (Wikipedia, 2013). It then moved slowly toward Greater Antilles and then on October 24th became a hurricane landing in Kingston Jamaica and then to the Caribbean Sea (Wikipedia, 2013). On October 25th, it hit Cuba as a Category 3 and then changed to Category 1(Wikipedia, 2013). On October 26th, it moved to the Bahamas (Wikipedia, 2013). On October 27th, it weakened to a tropical storm and then gained momentum and then changed to Category 1 Hurricane (Wikipedia, 2013).

On October 29th it changed course moving northwest and then stayed ashore near Brigantine New Jersey the Northeast of Atlantic City which then affected New York City (Wikipedia, 2013). The storm affected 24 States in the United States

Wall Street closed its doors during the Sandy Superstorm. Despite all the damages from the storm, Wall Street prepared to open doors for business on Wednesday after closing its market for two days. The N.Y.S.E, NASDAQ and other trading platforms returned normal operations following nonstop meetings and extensive testing of their systems. Wall Street folks feared a long delay would frustrate investors and tarnish their reputation. Upon opening it still had stacks of sand bags protecting the entrance to the New York Stock Exchange and Goldman Sachs. Electrical power was shut off for parts of the surrounding neighborhoods. Pockets of the financial district in lower Manhattan were still underwater when Wall Street resumed operations. Upon opening, Wall Street created an emergency mode of operation. In preparation, Wall Street created the emergency response team of about 30 staff members who slept in lower Manhattan headquarters. They advised firms and exchange trade groups what to do. The group, Security Industry and Financial Markets Association held one call with more than 400 regulators, exchange executives, traders and the New York City Officials.

Four months after Superstorm Sandy, historic district's businesses remained closed. Restaurants were still shut down due to faulty electrical systems all ruined by the storm. At least 1,000 jobs were lost in lower Manhattan of which 450 workers were in the Sea Port neighborhood. Brooklyn Bridge and the bridge café also had its share of nightmare of the storm. The bridge café endured economic ups and down including terrorist attacks. Its basement was flooded and water destroyed the building's wood foundation. Some Corporations were displaced for weeks after the storm and some employers and employees were relocated to temporary offices. Neighboring skyscrapers infrastructure and electrical systems that harbored Manhattan Financial Companies were also destroyed. Con Edison stated that 10 major buildings did not have power for several months and some were operating on emergency generators. 27 story office towers at 110 Wall Street near the Stock Exchange were badly damaged with floods. The building management now plans on constructing a structure to combat future storms. Phone and internet services hindered business activity when underground copper cables operated by Verizon the largest network provider were destroyed by the flood. By Mid-February, Verizon said only 10% of its customers had little service.

CHAPTER TEN

In conclusion the area is devastating and intriguing. It is only a little street however; it holds the key to New York City's wealth and esteem. According to Doug Henwood (1998), "Wall Street and its sister financial centers don't just influence government, effectively they are the government" (p. 1). No wonder, union organizations are commanvding power are now more interested in Wall Street and urging union workers to invest. Not only is it famous in New York but in the World as a financial district. "Together with Social Security, the UAW could rather smugly tell its members in the wake of a major Wall Street bear market in the early twenty-first century; these defined benefit plans are the rock-solid core of an approach that has been tested and proven for decades." (Sloane & Witney, 2010, p. 303). Once, you work close to the area, you could find investing interesting and would want to participate. Co-workers in the area always talk about stocks and investment; this is social networking and next thing you know, you are investing. Also Deferred Compensation; 401K and 457 have offices in that area. These are investment opportunities that workers in the city and some private job employees embark on to help individuals during retirement. Not only will one have pension but Deferred Compensation and Social Security. With these three or more investments in retirement, your future is guaranteed, and will make life easy during old age.

REFERENCES

Fineberg, T. 2013. "Sandy Storm News." *The Associate Press.* February (25).

Fraser, S. 2008. *Wall Street.* Yale University Press. New Haven. (Pages 139, 150-151 & 178)

Henwood, D. 1998. *Wall Street: How it works for whom.* USA.

Lendman, S. 2011. *How Wall Street Fleeces America: Privatized Banking. Government*

Collusion and Class War. USA.

Murolo, P. & Chitty. A. B., 2001. *From The Folks Who Brought You The Weekend.* The New

Press. New York. (Pages 125-127).

Nagy, R. A. & Obenberger, R. W. 1994. "Factors influencing individual investor behavior."

Financial Analysts Journal. 15(3):163-68

Sjoberg, K. 2004. "The Wall Street Culture." *European Journal of Cultural Studies 7(4): 481–499*

Sloane, A. A. & Witney, F.2010. *Labor Relations.* Prentice Hall. New Jersey. (Page 303)

Sultana, S. T. 2010. "An Empirical Study of Indian Individual Investors' Behavior" *Global*

Journal of Finance and Management. 19-33

Yao, M., Gutter, S. & Sherman D. 2010. "The Financial Risk Tolerance of Blacks,

Hispanics and Whites." *Survey of Consumer Finances.* 2(16):28-39

Wikipedia. 2013. "Hurricane Sandy as a Category 3: Hurricane on October 25, 2012." 2012. Time, October 29. Retrieved August 23. 2013. Wikipedia

www.ingramcontent.com/pod-product-compliance
Lightning Source LLC
Chambersburg PA
CBHW020758220326
41597CB00012BA/586